Jenny Kell
Paper Embellishment

Search Press

First published in Great Britain as *Paper Embellishment* 2005

Search Press Limited
Wellwood, North Farm Road,
Tunbridge Wells, Kent TN2 3DR

Originally published in 1999 as *Country Collage*

Text copyright © Jenny Kell 1999

Photographs by Search Press Studios
Photographs and design copyright © Search Press Ltd.
1999, 2005

ISBN 1 84448 067 4

Publisher's note

All the step-by-step photographs in this book feature the
author, Jenny Kell, demonstrating how to make pictures. No
models have been used.

It is the publishers' custom to recommend synthetic
materials as substitutes for animal products wherever
possible. There are now a large number of brushes available
made from artificial fibres and they are just as satisfactory as
those made from natural fibres.

*For William
and May*

*I would like to thank my family and
friends for their constant support and
encouragement.*

*Thanks are also due to Roz Dace,
Chantal Porter and Julie Wood,
together with everyone else at
Search Press, for all their help.*

*I would also like to thank the
following suppliers:
Crafty Arts at Brentwood,
Strand Gallery at Southend,
Sandra Turner at Wallington
and Richard Clarke at Romford.*

Printed in Malaysia by Times offset (M) Sdn Bhd

Contents

Introduction

Collage originated as a traditional folk art, but it was pioneered as a fine art in the early twentieth century by such innovators as Picasso and Georges Braque. They incorporated paper shapes into their paintings. Later on, Matisse and other artists went one step further and assembled collage pictures with no painting at all. Interest in this medium continued to grow as its versatility became recognised, and in recent times a seemingly endless variety of objects have been used to create interesting, and sometimes intensely personal, works of art.

I think my passion for collage developed as a natural result of my hoarding instincts. Ever since I can remember, I have collected 'useful' objects: fabrics, paper and card, shells and pebbles, interesting magazine articles, art materials, old herbals, maps and sheet music. I grew up in a family of keen (if chaotic) gardeners and was encouraged from an early age to take an interest in plants. So, I also accumulated a selection of pressed flowers. It was only when the spare room threatened to collapse under the weight of my hoarded clutter, that I decided something creative must be done with it all.

I began to categorise and study my collections and, from this, ideas for collages began to form in my mind. After a few rather stilted and formal attempts at botanical pictures, I began to experiment with a bolder, more random approach. I soon knew that I had found my own personal style.

You do not need any special artistic skills to master the art of collage – just an appreciation of colour and shape. Also, it is not an expensive craft – you will probably find many of the components in your own home and surroundings, or you will be able to buy them quite cheaply. The immediacy of this craft can effect fast and spontaneous results, yet a slower, more contemplative approach can be equally satisfying. Before being glued down, the

chosen components can be repositioned as often as wished, until the required overall impression is achieved. If you are dissatisfied, walk away and do something else for a few hours. When you come back, the problem areas may be seen more clearly, and corrected.

When searching for a new scene to form the basis of a collage, I always take my sketchbook with me to record colours, textures and other interesting details. However, it is the essence of a place that I wish to express rather than a photographic resemblance. I do spend a lot of time simply staring at a scene that interests me, hoping that it will be instilled into me, before carefully selecting the components that will be most evocative of the scene when I am recreating it back at my studio.

It can sometimes be difficult to describe things you do instinctively or routinely, and when I started to write this book I struggled for the appropriate words to express my working methods. As I progressed, however, I found the process of writing it all down both interesting and inspirational. It was rewarding to take time out from a busy work schedule to actually stop and think about what I was doing, and as I reflected upon one technique, other ideas would spring to mind.

By following the basic techniques of painting, positioning and gluing, I hope you will soon discover how easy it is to create your own collages. You may be inspired simply by your favourite colours, hobbies or places. Alternatively, your kitchen, garden or ideal holiday may provide the ideas you need. It is currently popular to create collages relating to dramatic events – both happy and sad – in ones life, and it is always great fun to make a collage to commemorate an important family celebration. In fact, there is an entire world of themes to choose from.

Materials

The materials you need to create collage pictures can be divided into simple categories: papers, fabrics, flowers and leaves, other collage items and basic materials.

The papers and fabrics are used to create backgrounds; and flowers and leaves can be glued on top. There are many items that can be used to embellish a collage further: buttons, seeds and dried fruit to name but a few. In addition, you will need a few simple materials to help you complete your collages: paints, brushes and glue, for example.

Although most of the materials can be found or bought inexpensively, it is worth investing in a few essential items such as good quality papers and art materials. Handmade papers can seem expensive but they will doubtless enhance your pictures. It is always best to buy the best quality art materials you can afford, but in many cases you may find that you can improvise.

You can save empty glass jars for use as water pots, and old saucers or china dishes make suitable mixing palettes.

There is a huge variety of paintbrushes available and this can be daunting. However, you will need only a small selection of brushes, mainly for backgrounds and adding detail. I always buy synthetic brushes – never sable. If washed thoroughly after use, you should find that these last a long time.

Papers

There are lots of wonderful papers and cards that can be used for collage pictures – the three basic types I use are listed below. In addition, I save tissue paper (plain white can be painted) and gift wrap. Maps, extracts of poetry, sheet music and printed articles could all be incorporated into a collage if they fit in with a theme. However, beware of copyright laws and restrictions if making pictures for commercial purposes.

Brown parcel paper and corrugated card can be incorporated into a picture with a natural theme, and even machine-made or office paper can be successfully used by tearing, cutting or painting it to fit in with a collage.

It is also possible to use your own photographs in collages. If you do not want to cut up an original, you can get it duplicated or colour photocopied.

Handmade paper

I use a heavy-duty paper for certain backgrounds. It has a rough, grainy texture which works particularly well with simple botanical-style pictures (see pages 40–41).

Watercolour paper

A rough paper is ideal for backgrounds. I use a heavy-duty paper that is more like card than paper and will not buckle when even the most vigorous colourwashes are applied.

I also use a thin watercolour paper which is excellent for torn-edge backgrounds (see page 28). This can be bought in spiral-bound pads.

Handmade tissue paper

This was once difficult to find, but it is now widely obtainable from good art shops. It is available in different thicknesses, and there is a huge variety of wonderful colours and textures to choose from.

Fabrics

I have hoarded lots of things over the years, including some of my old clothes. I vaguely thought that the material might come in useful one day. I can rarely pass a fabric shop without calling in to see if there is anything of interest, so I now have a large collection of materials to choose from.

Natural fibres, such as cotton, linen, silk and calico, work well with pressed flowers – these are all available in a variety of colours and designs.

It is often a piece of fabric which gives me the idea for a new collage. It may simply be the colour that I am interested in, or perhaps the texture. I generally tend to avoid fussily textured or patterned materials as I feel they detract from the delicate style of the flowers or the natural colours of the collage items, but, of course, there are exceptions to the rule.

I am always searching for contrast in my pictures, and fabrics can help to achieve this effect. I am, for example, particularly fond of blue and white checked or striped cotton – this can look stunning when used with vibrant yellow flowers.

You can achieve different effects with fabric by either cutting with sharp scissors for precise straight edges, or by simply tearing the fabric if you require a rougher, frayed effect.

Heavy fabrics can be fixed in position by brushing with glue, but care should be taken when working with finer fabrics. It is best to apply dots of glue using a cocktail stick . . . but beware – if you use too much glue, it will show through the fine material, but too little will prevent it from sticking down properly, causing it to lift when collage items are fixed on top. Always practise first.

Flowers & leaves

The choice of flowers suitable for pressing is enormous. The only real failures I have had are with very thick-petalled varieties, such as lilies or tulips.

I grow a selection of 'essential' flowers for pressing. Two that I would never be without are love-in-a-mist and larkspur – they both have an abundance of feathery green foliage and pink, white and blue flowerheads. I also like to introduce one or two new plants to the garden every year for variety and experimentation. I select plants, both for growing and pressing, on the basis of their colour and shape, and to gain as much contrast as possible.

I am constantly surprised at the large quantity of flowers that can be produced from even the smallest of gardens, like mine. However, for extra supplies you can also visit your local florist where you may discover new and unusual flowers to work with. The only rule to follow is to make sure that the flowers are really fresh and show no signs of wilting or damage.

Although I try to keep something in my presses all year round – even if it is only a few leaves and grasses – rain and snow and a scarcity of available flowers leads to a lack of activity during the winter months and it is always a pleasure to see the first snowdrops appear in early spring. During the summer, however, my presses are packed full and I am desperately seeking more space to squeeze in a few more irresistible perfect blooms.

The flowers shown on this page are the Iceland poppy, cowslip, rose, delphinium, French marigold, freesia, forget-me-not, pansy, kerria, verbena, rhododendron, lobelia, candytuft and larkspur. There is also a selection of leaves.

Other collage items

Most of my pictures are usually connected to
nature, the countryside and landscapes – these are
my particular passions. Gardens, woodlands,
beaches and meadows may be full of inspirational
items, but there are many other sources and themes
to choose from.

The kitchen can provide a good selection of
collage components – pressed herbs, spices, dried
beans, pulses, pasta, fruit and vegetables all make
colourful and aromatic ingredients. Slices of fruit
and vegetables must be dried rather than pressed. I
use specially designed racks for this, but you can
dry these slices successfully if you place them on
sheets of blotting paper and then leave them
outside on a sunny day. Alternatively, arrange them
on a baking tray and then place in the oven for
several hours on the lowest setting.

I have always been hugely inspired by the sea,
and many of my collage components tend to be
related to the shoreline. I spend many happy hours
searching for shells, pebbles and small pieces of
driftwood, but take only a few of each item – just
enough to enable me to try to recapture a scene
without feeling I have plundered it. I sometimes
use items such as starfish or sea urchins in my
pictures. However, if I use these, I always ensure
they are from an ecologically sound source – i.e.
they have been washed up on the beach rather than
having been deliberately harvested.

Once you begin to make collages, you too may
develop hoarding instincts and start to collect a vast
array of items. Later on, of course, you may not
want to choose any particular theme at all – you
may wish to create purely random, abstract pictures
– but it is a good starting point to reflect on the
subjects which most inspire you to achieve the
impressions you want.

Basic materials

Each project in this book includes a specific list of the items required . It is a good idea to read this list carefully before you begin.

1. **Water-based paints** I use tubes of artists' quality paint for large washes, and pans for more intricate details.

2. **Palette** Paints should be mixed in a palette. It is best to choose one with deep wells as these are useful for mixing up washes.

3. **Water jar** For rinsing brushes and adding water for washes.

4. **Watercolour paintbrushes** A large wash brush is needed for creating flat watercolour washes. A large round brush, however, will be more versatile when filling in smaller areas (see page 26). A medium round brush will be useful for some paint effects (see page 27) and more detailed work. Finally, a small round brush is handy for adding finer details.

5. **Eraser** For erasing pencil marks.

6. **Pencil** An HB pencil is useful for making rough sketches when planning a design and for drawing borders.

7. **Waterproof pigment pens** For writing on pictures (see page 41). These can also be used for labelling packets of flowers. Permanent markers are also suitable but they do not dry as quickly and, although described as permanent, some can still fade over time.

8. **Scissors** For cutting card and fabric. It is best to use small scissors for trimming delicate flowers and leaves.

9. **Tweezers** For handling delicate pressed flowers and moving them into position.

10. **Absorbent paper** For mopping up spills and for removing excess paint from the brush (see page 25). It can also be used instead of a natural sponge to create cloud effects (see page 36).

11. **Masking tape** I use 2.5cm (1in) tape for marking borders and for creating pattern effects in watercolour backgrounds (see pages 26–27).

12. **Ready-cut card mount** This is used as a guide when planning collages or creating borders. The mount can be placed over your picture to check that edges are straight and angles are correct in a composition. Also, a pencil line drawn around the mount will give you a rectangular border.

13. **Clear-faced bags** For storing pressed flowers and collage items.

14. **Sticky labels** For labelling bags of pressed flowers.

15. **Ruler** For drawing in borders and measuring.

16. **Hot glue gun** For sticking down certain collage items (particularly three-dimensional objects) on to a background This is messy and should be used with care.

17. **PVA glue** For gluing paper, card, fabric, flowers and leaves. Rubber solution glue can also be used.

18. **Cocktail sticks** For applying glue to flowers, leaves, thin fabric, paper or tissue.

19. **Masking fluid** For masking off areas from paint. Rubber solution glue can be used instead of masking fluid.

20. **Toothbrush** For flicking and splattering masking fluid to create interesting patterns and effects in backgrounds (see page 26).

21. **Glue brush** For applying glue to card, thick paper or thick fabric.

22. **Flower press** For pressing flowers and leaves.

Note A slope-topped desk easel is an extremely useful item which can be purchased quite inexpensively from art shops. Although not essential, it will provide a good working surface for watercolour washes, allowing the paint to flow gently down the sheet. (A simple alternative could be made by propping a wooden board against several heavy books.) Also, if space is limited in your home, paints, brushes and other materials can be stored inside the desk. The desk is fully portable and can be carried to any convenient spot. The wooden top can be protected with sheets of blotting paper or newspaper.

I use the slope-topped desk easel for watercolour washes, but transfer the work to a flat surface for laying out and gluing in place the flowers and other collage components.

Getting organised

It is important to keep materials organised, particularly pressed flowers. You will find that this will make it much easier when it comes to creating your collages.

Office card index drawers make excellent storage units for packets of pressed flowers and leaves (but shoe boxes or plain wooden boxes would do). Pressed flowers can be placed in clear-faced bags and then labelled, and a titled index card system will enable you to then file the flowers – this will help you to quickly find the exact flower you require, instead of sifting through a jumble of assorted ones. Keeping flowers organised in this way will also help protect them from damage.

Larger flowers or long-stemmed varieties can be laid between sheets of blotting paper and weighted down with heavy books until ready for use.

I find it very useful to pin fabric, paper and other scraps on to a cork notice board during the early planning stages of a collage. It enables me to see at a glance whether the colour scheme I have chosen is working, and whether I have assembled enough suitable components. I can also add to the collection whenever a suitable item is found. I may leave the selection of items pinned to the board for several weeks before actually starting to make the new picture. During this time, I study it frequently to decide how it could be improved upon.

A card index drawer is ideal for storing and organising flowers and leaves.

Opposite
Fabric and paper samples can be pinned on to a cork noticeboard and arranged according to colour, texture or pattern. It is also a good idea to pin up any reference notes and reminders or scribbled ideas on themes for future collages.

Preparation

Flowers and leaves need to be pressed carefully before you can use them in a collage. Pressing flowers is a rewarding activity. It can be time-consuming but if you are unable to press your own flowers, there are specialist suppliers who can provide you with them.

I believe the spirit of a picture is established by the background and I always try hard to avoid dull, flat or boring backgrounds. I love experimenting with different colours and mediums to create interesting and original scenes and, wherever possible, I try to give an impression of 'light'. In this section, I show you how to create some simple yet effective backgrounds. The basic techniques are straight-forward and easy to follow, allowing great freedom for creativity. No special artistic drawing skills are required and you can experiment with any number of different mediums to achieve the results you are looking for. You can adapt these basic techniques to create your own unique backgrounds. When you are planning your pictures, it is worth spending time thinking about the backgrounds and trying out various effects – if you are not satisfied, you can always start again.

Pressing flowers

You can buy a flower press from craft or art shops, or you can make your own (see below and opposite).

    The time needed for flowers to dry will vary depending on the thickness of the petals, but as a general rule, small flowers will require approximately three weeks and flowers with thicker petals will take about six weeks. Flowers should only be removed from the press when they feel dry and papery to the touch. Always handle pressed plant material with care to avoid damaging fragile petals and leaves.

 Many species of wild flower are protected, so always check before you pick them.

 Even if a wild plant is not protected, it is kinder to select only a few flower heads, leaving enough for the flower to flourish in the future.

 Always pick flowers on a dry, warm day after all the dew has evaporated. Pick only perfect blooms, preferably just after a bud has opened.

Making a flower press

It is simple to make a homemade press, and this will enable you to dry quite a few flowers at a time. A homemade press has the advantage that it can be made to any size you choose, and it can accommodate whole flower stems, or enough flower heads to make a pressing session worthwhile.

A homemade press is made using layers of single-corrugated card, blotting paper and tissue paper. Corrugated card is an essential component of the flower press as it allows air to circulate between layers – this aids the drying process and prevents the flowers from going brown. Try to find a type which has thick, flat outer edges, otherwise the corrugated lines may appear on the pressed flowers.

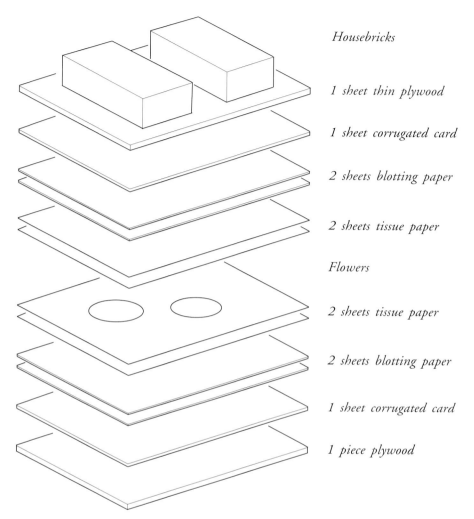

Housebricks

1 sheet thin plywood

1 sheet corrugated card

2 sheets blotting paper

2 sheets tissue paper

Flowers

2 sheets tissue paper

2 sheets blotting paper

1 sheet corrugated card

1 piece plywood

You Will Need
2 sheets of 6mm (¼in) plywood
Sheets of single-corrugated cardboard
Sheets of blotting paper
Sheets of tissue paper
Heavy books or house bricks

Flowers can be sandwiched in between single-corrugated card, blotting paper and tissue paper. This sandwich effect can be repeated and layers built up to include lots of flowers. When complete, the sandwich should be placed between two sheets of plywood and weighted down with heavy books or house bricks. Alternatively, you could drill holes in each corner of the press and secure with screws and wing nuts. If you want to do this, ensure that the plywood is slightly bigger than the sandwich, to allow the screws to go through.

Opposite
Flower presses can be bought from craft or art shops, or a simple one can be made using a large book, some paper tissues and a housebrick. This type of press, however, is limited and is only suitable for pressing small, thin flowers. It is not recommended for regular use.

Creating backgrounds

I always place huge importance on – and have great fun with – backgrounds. I work my washes on a sloping desk easel, but you could use a piece of board supported by books. If you experiment with washes, you may find that you can work successfully on a flat surface.

Flat wash

You can use any colour for a flat wash, but this demonstration is worked with blue. Different colours can be mixed together to create the exact tone you require, and the density of the colour can be altered by controlling the amount of water added to the paint in the mixing palette. Remember that whatever colour you use, it will appear slightly lighter when dry.

You Will Need
Water-based paint
Large wash or round brush
Scrap paper
Heavy-duty watercolour paper
Absorbent paper
Palette
Water jar

1. Squeeze a small amount of paint into a palette. Add sufficient water to give the colour value you want, and mix thoroughly. Test the colour on a piece of scrap paper.

2. Place the watercolour paper on a sloping board. Load a large wash or round brush with colour then lay down a brushstroke at the top of the paper.

3. Load the brush again and paint a second brushstroke underneath the first, blending as you work. Repeat to complete the wash. Work fairly quickly to prevent the pools of paint at the bottom of each stroke from drying and forming hard edges.

4. When you have completed the wash, wipe the brush on absorbent paper and stroke it along the bottom edge of the watercolour paper to collect the residue of wet paint. Leave to dry on a flat surface.

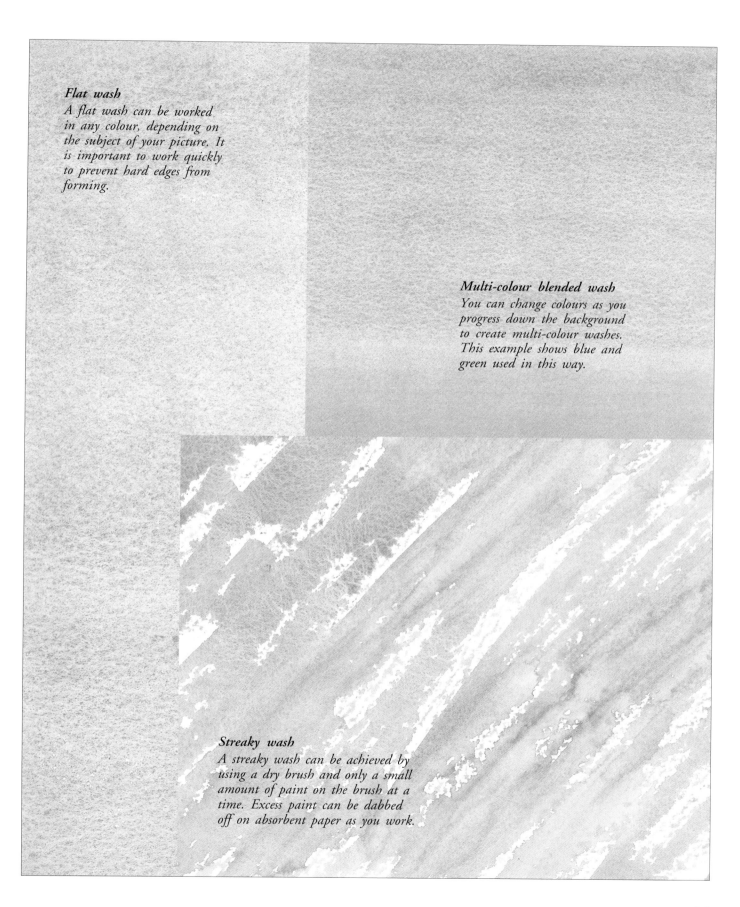

Flat wash
A flat wash can be worked in any colour, depending on the subject of your picture. It is important to work quickly to prevent hard edges from forming.

Multi-colour blended wash
You can change colours as you progress down the background to create multi-colour washes. This example shows blue and green used in this way.

Streaky wash
A streaky wash can be achieved by using a dry brush and only a small amount of paint on the brush at a time. Excess paint can be dabbed off on absorbent paper as you work.

25

Masked colour wash

Masking tape and fluid can be used to create different effects by exposing the background paper. Tape can produce hard edges and the impression of rays or streaks of light. Masking fluid can be dropped on with a brush or flicked and splattered using a toothbrush, to create pin pricks or splatters of light.

You Will Need

Heavy-duty watercolour paper
2.5cm (1in) masking tape
Masking fluid
Old toothbrush
Large wash or round brush
Medium round brush
Water-based paints: blue, green and yellow
Water jar

1. Apply strips of masking tape to the paper.

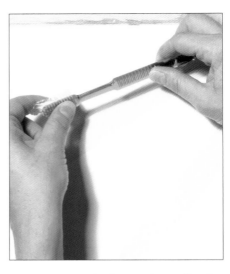

2. Splatter a little masking fluid over the paper using an old toothbrush. Allow to dry.

3. Decant yellow paint into a palette and add a little water. Repeat with blue and green. Use a large wash or round brush to paint random patches of yellow and blue. Allow the colours to run and merge to create backruns. Do not leave to dry.

4. Paint green into the remaining white areas, and again allow all the colours to blend on the paper. Leave until almost dry.

5. Use a medium round brush to drop clean water into a small area of the drying paint – this will create further patterns and abstract shapes. Leave to dry.

6. Remove the masking tape carefully.

7. Gently rub away the masking fluid with your finger.

8. Fill in the blank areas left by the masking tape with more blue and green merged washes. Leave the white areas left by the masking fluid to represent sparkles of light.

The finished wash
This striking background uses masking tape and masking fluid to create the effect of rays and pin pricks of light. A multi-coloured wash adds to the atmosphere of the background.

Torn-edge wash

Watercolour paper can be torn to create an interesting and lively edge. Care should be taken to work the paint well into the edges to avoid any gaps.

You Will Need

Thin watercolour paper
Heavy-duty watercolour paper
Water-based paint: blue and green
Large round brush
PVA glue and glue brush
Water jar
Palette

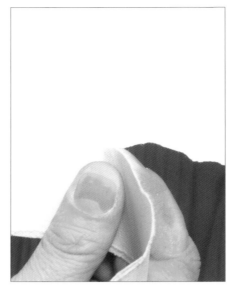

1. Tear around the edges of the thin watercolour paper. Tear towards yourself, so that you can see and control the rough edge.

2. Mix blue paint with water to create a pale wash. Apply random patches of colour over the thin watercolour paper. Repeat with a pale green wash.

3. Paint right into the torn edges using blue and green washes. Leave to dry. Brush PVA glue over the back of the painted paper. Press this carefully on to a sheet of heavy-duty watercolour paper, leaving an even border all the way around.

The finished collage
A rough torn edge and unmerged colours can create an interesting background.

Random collage background

Scraps of fabric and torn pieces of handmade paper or tissue paper can be used to create an abstract impression or to suggest a scene. Colour can be used to great effect – for example, warm, earthy tones with deep reds and oranges are ideal for an autumnal picture, and pale greens and yellows suggest a spring scene.

You can further decorate areas of collage where more detail is needed by applying dots or swirls of paint (see page 51).

All the backgrounds on this page are made using a collage of torn paper and fabric.

Projects

There is no limit to the number of different pictures you can create with collage. This section takes you through just some of the possibilities. I hope that it will inspire you to come up with ideas of your own.

I have not given exact dimensions for background papers for each project – this is largely up to you, and will depend upon the quantity of flowers you have available, and the size you want your finished piece to be.

When you are ready to begin making your pictures and have assembled all your collage pieces together, you may find it useful to lay out all the components on a spare piece of paper. You can then arrange and rearrange the items until you feel satisfied with your design.

When you feel confident to begin working out your own collages, care should be taken with composition. You will find it easier if you have a basic design in mind before you begin, and it is a good idea to make some rough sketches for this. My list of collage ideas for future pictures includes a herb garden, country remedies, samplers and countries (based on items I have collected on my travels through Europe). I am also planning a huge collage featuring the shipping forecast. The scope is truly endless.

Larkspur

You can press individual florets of larkspur or whole stems. The latter are rather bulky, but they press surprisingly well. I usually use several different flowers in one picture, but larkspur stems justify a picture all of their own. Try working different backgrounds to alter the effect.

You Will Need

Stems of pressed larkspur
Heavy-duty watercolour paper: white
Masking tape, 2.5cm (1in)
Large wash brush
Water-based paint: blue
Cocktail stick
Tweezers
PVA glue
Palette
Water jar

1. Use 2.5cm (1in) masking tape to mask off a border around the sides and top of the paper. Place a strip at the bottom of the paper, approximately 0.5cm (¼in) up from the edge.

2. Mix up a blue wash. Use a dry brush and a small amount of colour to apply a streaky wash diagonally across the paper (see page 25). Leave to dry.

3. Remove the masking tape from the background. Use the tip of a cocktail stick to transfer tiny dots of PVA glue to the back of each flower head and stem.

4. Use tweezers to pick up each flower carefully and position it over the background. Press gently into place.

Note Use only tiny pin pricks of glue to fix flowers to the collage – too much glue will squeeze out when the flower is pressed on to the paper. Sometimes, this can be gently rubbed away with your finger, but this may cause damage to delicate petals.

Larkspur
Pink larkspur stems are used against a blue streaky wash to produce a striking,
but simple picture. A variety of watercolour backgrounds and flowers could be
used in this style of picture.

Love-in-a-mist

Love-in-a-mist is available in shades of pink, white and blue. By using only one of the colours on its own, you can make a single statement, drawing attention to the flowers. The green and blue tones in this background wash are used to further emphasise the whiteness of the flowers.

Rain daisy

Osteospermums *are lovely to use but inevitably – however careful you are – a few petals will fall off when they are removed from the press. When I discovered their common name was 'Rain Daisy' I thought I would use their falling petals to suggest rain drops. A grey and blue streaky wash is used for the cloudy sky, and drops of clear water are added when the paint is almost dry, to form backruns for an overall watery effect.*

Flower garden

For this project, I wanted to convey nature's energy, with plants of all colours and types thriving. I have cheated a little by showing all the flowers out in full bloom at the same time in order to convey the impression I wanted.

1. Mix up a blue wash then paint the background using a large wash brush. Create clouds by dabbing the wet wash with absorbent paper. Leave to dry.

2. Apply glue to the anemones and then position them in the centre of the background (see page 32). Press in place.

3. Work in the aubrieta, lobelia and michaelmas daisies behind the anemones. Try to get the design symmetrical.

4. Insert a selection of leaves into the foreground.

5. Fill in the middle foreground with roses, astrantia, delphiniums, larkspur and love-in-a-mist.

6. Fill in any small spaces using verbena and common daisies.

7. Trim the ends of the leaves at the bottom of the picture using a pair of scissors.

Flower garden
Anemones are always colourful and eyecatching – once the central flowers are in place you can build up the rest of the picture around them.

Spring meadow
Spring flowers are used to represent a wildflower meadow. The flowers featured
in this picture are cornflowers, larkspur, buttercups, common daisies, rain daisies
(or cape marigolds) and candytuft. A masked colour wash (see pages 26–27) adds
interest to the background.

Poppy field
I have tried to convey the fragile beauty of poppies in this picture. A masked
colour wash (see pages 26–27) is used to capture the atmosphere of summer.

38

Botanical

I have used a rough, heavily-textured handmade paper for the central rectangle of this picture to provide a lovely contrast with the delicate petals of the flowers. The edges are touched with purple water-based paint to make them stand out against the plain background sheet. You could use this type of picture to keep a record of the plants you grow, perhaps even tying several sheets together to form a journal!

You Will Need

Pressed flowers: aubrieta, bidens, michaelmas daisies, candytuft, cinquefoil, delphinium, forget-me-not, lobelia, love-in-a-mist, pansy, rose and French marigold

Heavy-duty watercolour paper: white

Rough-textured heavy-duty handmade paper: white

Medium round paintbrush

Water-based paint: dark purple

Pencil and eraser

Ruler

PVA glue and glue brush

Cocktail stick

Tweezers

Palette

Water jar

Waterproof pigment pen

1. Pencil in a border around the edge of the watercolour paper, approximately 2.5cm (1in) in from the edge.

2. Arrange michaelmas daisies around the border. Try to get the stems following the pencilled line. Stick in place with PVA glue. Erase any visible pencil lines.

3. Tear a rectangle from hand-made paper to fit inside the flower border. Use a medium round paintbrush to paint the edges of the rectangle dark purple. Leave to dry.

4. Brush the back of the rectangle with PVA glue and press into position in the middle of the background.

5. Position a delphinium in the centre of the rectangle then glue it in place.

6. Position the rest of the flowers. Play with the design until you are happy with it, then glue the flowers into position. Write in the names of the flowers using a waterproof pigment pen.

forget-me-not

rose

bidens

love-in-a-mist

French marigold

pansy

aubrieta

delphinium

lobelia

candytuft

cinquefoil

Botanical
Michaelmas daisies frame this picture. An additional border is created by
painting the edges of the handmade paper with dark purple water-based paint.

Roses and love-in-a-mist

The border in this collage is created to reflect the way in which roses and love-in-a-mist grow entwined together in my garden. Torn watercolour paper is painted pale blue for the central panel and a small bouquet of the flowers is positioned on top.

Ferns and flowers

A border of colourful flowers and leaves is created, and a pale green flat wash is painted over the whole of the middle section of torn watercolour paper. This provides the background against which the individual flowers are displayed.

43

Country flowers

The dark green handmade tissue paper used in this project provides a good background contrast for the flowers. I have chosen brightly coloured and white flowers, as dark ones would get lost against the green background. You could experiment with different coloured papers and flowers.

You Will Need

Pressed flowers: alyssum, astrantia, bidens, cinquefoil, common daisy, delphinium, freesia, hydrangea, larkspur, love-in-a-mist, pansy and rose
Heavy-duty handmade paper: white
Handmade tissue paper: dark green
PVA glue
Cocktail stick
Tweezers
Waterproof pigment pen

1. Fold the green tissue paper into strips roughly 2.5cm (1in) wide. Tear along the folds to form strips.

2. Fold each strip into squares and then tear out twelve squares.

3. Arrange the green squares on the handmade paper, then glue in place.

4. Position the pressed flowers on the green squares. Experiment with the design until you are happy with it, then glue the flowers in place.

Country flowers
Brightly coloured and white flowers are displayed to good effect against contrasting dark green tissue squares. You can write the names of the plants on the completed picture if you wish. Use a waterproof pigment pen for this.

alyssum

cinquefoil

rose

astrantia

love-in-a-mist

bidens

larkspur

freesia

common daisy

pansy

delphinium

hydrangea

Orange squares
Layers of contrasting handmade papers can add depth and interest to a collage. Here,
I have used orange and beige textured papers to contrast with simple pale flowers.
You could try any variety of layers and colours to create different effects.

Summer flowers
The lovely ragged edges formed by tearing thin blue tissue paper contrast
well with the textured white paper on top. Bright summer flowers are then
displayed to their best effect on top of each layered square.

46

Daisies

This project introduces the use of fabric in a collage. Blue and white checked and striped fabrics are cut into small rectangles, and these are positioned on top of a background of handmade tissue paper. You can use this technique to make a variety of collage backgrounds.

You Will Need

Pressed flowers: oxeye, michaelmas, common and rain daisies

Heavy-duty watercolour paper: white

Handmade tissue paper: blue and yellow

Water-based paint: blue

Large round brush

Odd pieces of blue fabric

PVA glue and glue brush

Tweezers and cocktail stick

Sharp scissors

Palette

Water jar

1. Cut out three different size rectangles of fabric. Tear out one blue and one yellow rectangle of handmade tissue paper to create the background.

2. Arrange the rectangles of tissue paper on the watercolour paper, leaving a small border. Glue in place then arrange and glue the fabric pieces on top.

3. Tear a fresh piece of watercolour paper into three squares and/or rectangles. Apply a blue wash to each piece. Leave to dry.

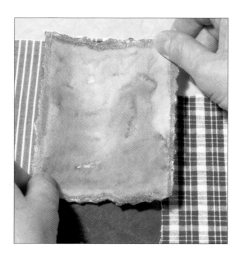

4. Place the colourwashed paper on the collage. Experiment until you are happy with the position then glue in place.

5. Arrange daisies on the collaged background. When you are pleased with the design, glue the flowers in place.

Daisy collage

The inspiration for this collage came from seeing a meadow of oxeye daisies. I have included other types of daisy – michaelmas, common and rain – to add additional splashes of colour. The yellow and blue colour scheme works well with the daisies, and the overall effect is bright and cheerful.

Pot marigolds

Pot marigold petals have a lovely silky sheen when pressed. Matt dark blue and orange paper and small scraps of pale blue fabric are used to contrast with the shiny flowers. A few swirls and spots of white paint add the final decoration.

Roses

A multi-coloured streaky watercolour border is painted and the colours are allowed to run into each other at the corners. Once this is dry, streaks of white paint are added to the border. A rectangle of fabric is placed in the centre and roses are arranged on top. Finally, rosebuds are placed in a border to frame the picture.

51

Seaside

Whenever I go on holiday, I always return home with masses of ideas for new pictures. Most of the components of this collage were collected, or bought, on these visits – even the fabrics were from shirts I bought whilst on holiday and then accidentally shrunk in the wash!

If you do not want to use original photographs, you can get them colour photocopied, or you can order duplicates from the negatives.

You Will Need

Pressed flowers: astrantia, bidens, michaelmas daisies, thrift and violets

Starfish, shells and driftwood

Holiday photographs

Heavy-duty watercolour paper: white

Handmade tissue paper: blue and yellow

Heavy-duty handmade paper: cream

Odd pieces of blue and yellow fabric in various patterns

Sharp scissors

PVA glue and hot glue gun

Glue brush and cocktail stick

Tweezers

1. Cut out pieces of blue and yellow fabric and tear the handmade paper and tissue paper into squares and rectangles of varying sizes. Arrange the pieces on the watercolour paper. Apply PVA glue to the back of each piece and press into place.

Note Apply glue to thick pieces of fabric and paper using a glue brush; use a cocktail stick for thin pieces.

2. Tear around the edges of the photographs. Brush the back of each piece with PVA glue and press in place.

3. Position the starfish, shells and driftwood. Glue in place using a hot glue gun.

4. Position the violets, michaelmas daisies, thrift, astrantia and bidens in the gaps. Stick in place with PVA glue.

Seaside

An abstract background is composed with paper and fabric, then other collage components are arranged on top. This style of collage is perfect for displaying a collection of holiday memories.

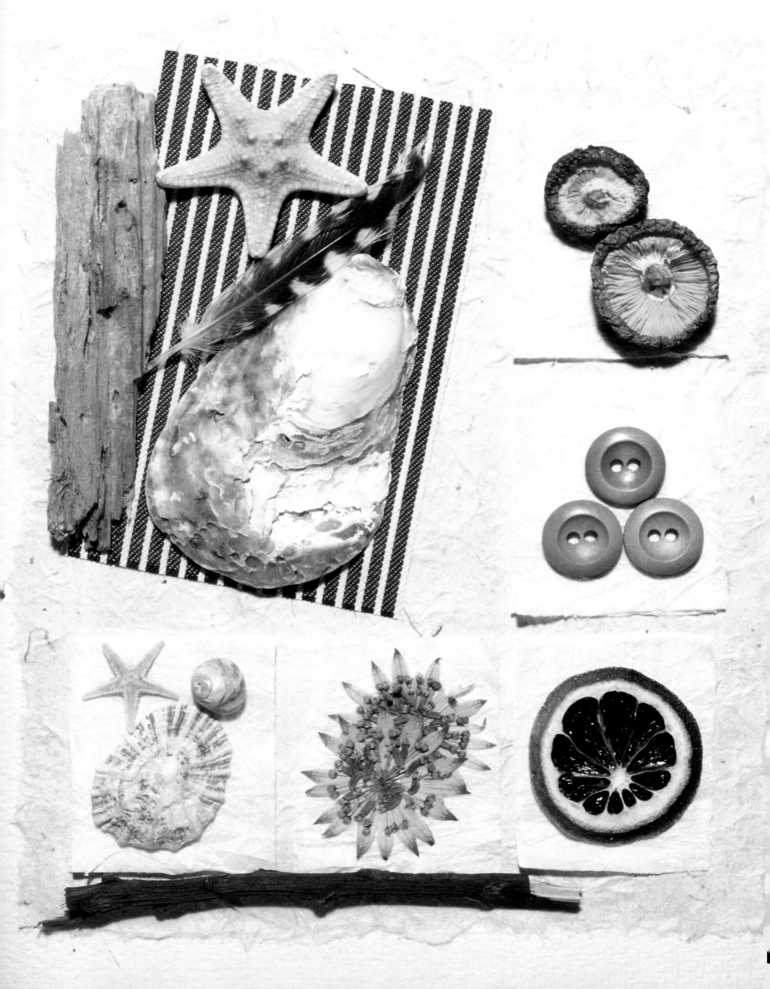

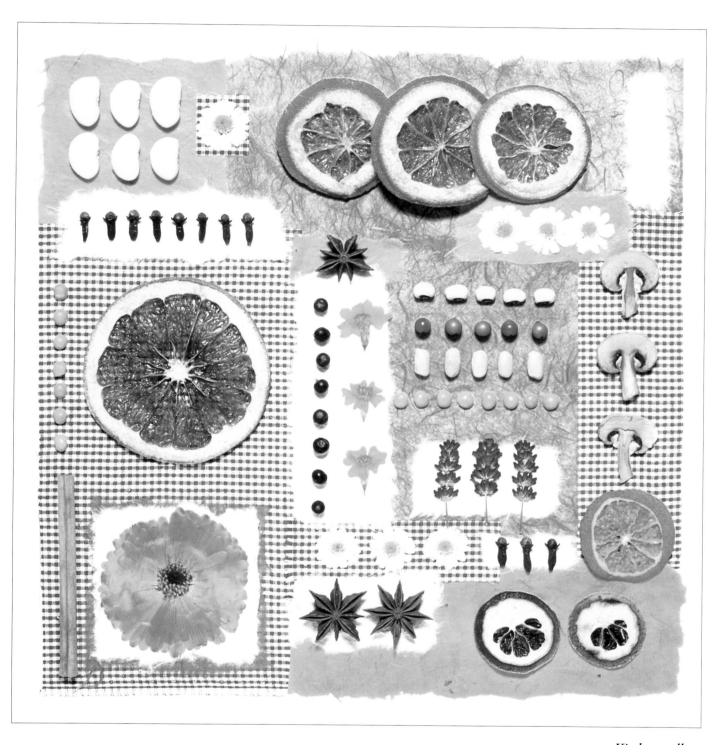

Kitchen collage
Kitchen collages are particular favourites of mine. Here, I have used dried beans, pulses and berries, dried slices of mushrooms, oranges and limes, pressed herbs (lavender, pot marigold and feverfew) and spices (cinnamon stick, cloves and star anise).

Nature
A collection of items can be grouped together and incorporated into a 'natural' collage. In this picture, I have used shells, starfish, a piece of driftwood, a feather, a twig, wooden buttons, a pressed astrantia, dried mushrooms and a slice of dried lime.

Jug of anemones

I wanted to make a still-life type of collage and chose anemones because I liked the dramatic effect of their vivid colours against the pale background wash. You can either draw the jug freehand, or photocopy the pattern provided, enlarging it to whatever size you want. You can then trace it on to watercolour paper.

You Will Need

Pressed flowers: anemones and anemone leaves

Heavy-duty watercolour paper: white

Thin watercolour paper: white

Piece of blue checked fabric

Water-based paint: blue and green

Sharp scissors

2.5cm (1in) masking tape

Large wash or round brush

Medium round brush

Palette and water jar

PVA glue and glue brush

Cocktail stick

Tweezers

Pattern for the jug

1. Apply masking tape around the edges of the heavy-duty watercolour paper to create a border. Work a very pale blue and green blended wash over the background (see page 25). Leave to dry. Remove the masking tape.

2. Cut out a piece of checked fabric and glue in place on the background to represent a tablecloth.

3. Cut the shape of a jug from thin watercolour paper. Paint blue spots on it using a medium round brush. Leave to dry and glue in place.

4. Arrange the anemones and leaves. Apply glue to the centres of the anemones only. Overlap the leaves and press into place.

Jug of anemones
A jug is cut out from watercolour paper and decorated with blue spots. The anemones are allowed to overlap the edges of the jug to give a more realistic feel to the design. The use of fabric to represent a tablecloth is very effective in this still life.

Yellow vase
Yellow marbled paper is used for this vase and a bunch of cornflowers and daisies are arranged in it. Some of the flowers are positioned spilling out of the vase, to make the design look more natural.

Pot of pansies
A pale blue and green blended wash is painted for the background and terracotta tissue paper is used for the flower pot. Various shades of pansy are positioned, with some overlapping the edges of the pot. Moss is glued in position to add the finishing touch.

59

Framing

Finished collages will be enhanced and protected from dust and damage if mounted and framed. Good art shops carry a wide selection of mounts and frame mouldings to choose from. Try to pick styles and colours which will compliment your pictures. Alternatively, look for plain wooden frames which you can then paint yourself in the colours you require.

A mount often finishes off a picture, but it also ensures that the glass is kept clear of the collage – this is particularly important if you are working with dried flowers which, although pressed, still have a certain amount of depth – you do not want to display them squashed up against glass!

For collages which use three-dimensional components, you will need to display your work in a box frame. Box frames are widely available from frame suppliers, but you could turn an everyday frame into a box frame.

Handpainted frame
This frame was originally a plain wooden one. I painted it first with two coats of white emulsion then, when this was dry, with a touch of blue emulsion on a dry brush. I chose a contrasting dark blue mount to make the picture stand out.

Antique-effect frame
The moulding used for this frame is distressed during manufacture to give it an antique look.

Limed frame

This frame tones in with the colours of the handmade tissue paper squares without detracting from them. The wood has been limed to lighten the wood and give an antique effect.

Pre-painted frame

Pre-painted frames are available in a range of colours. The dark green mount in this picture matches the handmade tissue paper, and the lighter green frame is used as a contrast.

62

Box frame
A driftwood-style box frame enhances the natural theme of this shell, starfish and flower collage.

Index